Minimalism

A Pragmatic Manual For Streamlining Your Living Space And Personal Life, Managing Your Finances To Cultivate Happiness, Well-Being, And Balance Using Established Minimalist Techniques Designed For Families

(A Concise Manual For Minimizing Waste And Economizing)

Pablo Benavente

TABLE OF CONTENT

Methods for Decluttering 1

The Advantages Of Having Only What You Need 12

Take Up a Method 41

Myths About Minimalism 62

Obtain Mental Clarity 111

Methods for Decluttering

Organizing consultant Marie Kondo described the steps involved in tidying up as putting your hands on everything you own, asking yourself if it makes you happy, and deciding whether to keep or discard it. After you've made your decision about what to preserve, you need to make sure it's easily visible and accessible.

Most individuals deal with the largest issue of discarding valuable items, whether they are sentimental, monetary, or real. Is it anything you use? is the crucial question. If not, it's probably best to eliminate it because you probably don't need it. This can be more difficult in certain situations, such as when the item has a high market worth, where you might decide to sell it. Many expensive items are worthless when you try to sell them, indicating that they aren't valuable and you can part with them.

And the sentimental items—what about them? You'll have to make your own decision on this, but you should make sure it's something that makes your life better. Examples of such items are pens you received as gifts or pictures of you with pals. Items you can let go of, such as the stack of photo albums you seldom look at or the gifts you never liked but never felt you could throw away, are dangerous. If the memories are still important to you, scan the pictures so you always have a duplicate in case you wish to look at them later.

Tips for Decluttering

Here are some of my suggestions for organizing and decluttering your possessions. In this section, you will discover how to handle sentimental items and organize your closet. You'll also pick up more effective life organization skills. We'll talk more about these subjects later in the book. Nevertheless, bear in mind the following guidelines:

Consider organizing by category.

Others believe that organizing your belongings per room is more effective. They sort the things in each room of their houses. The truth is that it differs from person to person. Decluttering by category can prove to be more effective for you. Sort your possessions into categories.

You may, for instance, assemble all of your books and decide which ones to keep and which to discard. Kondo suggests that since clothes are the least emotionally charged item, you start with them. After that, you ought to proceed to books and pictures.

Initially, work with level surfaces.

If your home is anything like mine, there is no such thing as a clean surface. Whenever I see an unoccupied table, I always set something down on it. Selecting a level surface to tidy, like a floor, shelf, tabletop, or countertop, is a smart first step. Pay attention to this field. Arrange your belongings in a pile and begin organizing them. Wait until you're done with one region before moving on to another.

Put nostalgia out of your mind.

Many people treasure their possessions for their sentimental meaning. They frequently save old pictures, souvenirs from trips, friend postcards, vintage toys from their youth, etc. Put aside your nostalgia and adopt a rational and useful mindset. Remember that while you can always treasure the memories, you do not need to save every object connected to them.

Toss it aside

You'll quickly discover that purging is enjoyable. Kondo suggests assembling all of your clothing and stacking it. After that, you should decide which ones to keep. If you could wear the same 20% of your items 80% of the time, you would only need a fifth of your wardrobe. Consider what you wear daily. You can see how this would provide more space and be considerably less expensive.

Sort and arrange your clothes.

I know this sounds extreme, but just be patient with me. Make a pile of everything you take out of your closet. After that, separate them into three heaps by sorting them. Clothes that you can give to charities should make up the first one. The items in the second one ought to be ones you can sell. The third pile you should or don't mind tossing away is the pile.

Check your clothing thoroughly. Place items in any pile you haven't worn in the last six months. Retain the ones you truly value and find appealing. After that, return your clothing to the closet. Sort them into neat rows based on type. You can simply obtain the things you need in this way.

Additionally, you will have less time to decide what to dress if you have fewer options. You will have more time and energy to devote to more significant things. You might even want to think about dressing the same way every day, like Mark Zuckerberg, the creator of Facebook, does.

Decide to fold instead of hanging.

After sorting through the ones you must discard, you must pick where to place the items you have chosen to keep. Consider keeping your clothes folded and stored in a dresser.

Arrange your clothing in a vertical fold.

Try folding your items vertically to make your belongings more organized and conserve room. This is especially helpful because it allows you to view every item of clothing you own at once, rather than having to search through several items piled on top of one another. Additionally, it keeps you from creating a mess whenever you need to buy shirts. You can just pull it out rather than dig it out from under a heap of other clothes and utterly disarray the place. Clothes folded vertically will resemble origami pieces made of fabric. You can arrange them inside your dresser in orderly rows.

I would also suggest dividing your drawers with shoeboxes or cartons. You may keep your folded clothes upright in this manner. Additionally, you can use deep boxes for sweaters and compact boxes for square scarves.

Put your wallet in order.

Empty your wallet and place all of your belongings on a table. Arrange the following: coins, cash, pictures, receipts, cards, etc. Get rid of everything you don't need, including outdated invoices.

Loyalty cards are among the ones you should keep in a drawer or box when not in use. Lastly, reseal your wallet with cash, credit, and business cards.

What Takes Place UponDecluttering?

You'll see noticeable improvements in your daily routine and organizing habits in just a few weeks. For example:

You'll realize that getting dressed is no longer a stressful task.

You won't have to go through the heaps of clothing in your closet anymore because it is now arranged. Everything is perfectly visible to you. Your closet isn't filled, so you have ample space to move around. Additionally, you'll be happier since you'll genuinely value everything you've chosen to retain. You can relieve the burden of constantly developing new wardrobe ideas when you have fewer options.

You'll be able to identify your true interests.

An excessive amount of clothing might be confusing. It may be challenging to decide what to wear because of the variety and clashing trends. It will be much simpler to identify your style if you empty your closet and only keep the items that make you happy. You'll find it simpler to mix and match items and look for clothing later.

You'll choose quality before quantity.

When you have a large wardrobe, you pay attention to each item's appeal, style, design, and color. As previously indicated, you'll spend a lot less if you can reduce your wardrobe to the items you wear daily, allowing you to purchase higher-quality items. Superior fabrics and materials give clothing a longer lifespan. Also, classic pieces are always in vogue, so you should choose them. In the ensuing years, you can still wear them. To stay current, you can also mix them with trendy items. You don't need to purchase a lot of new clothing.

Although we've only discussed clothes thus far, these ideas apply to practically every aspect of your life.

The Advantages Of Having Only What You Need

When many people hear the phrase minimalism, they often only associate it with decluttering their homes, although it encompasses much more. It teaches you to let go of limiting behaviors and attitudes that you might be clinging to in addition to material possessions.

The Incredible Advantages of Living a Simple Life

It's time to go over some advantages of this new way of living if you're still not convinced by the joys of minimalism. What benefits might this genuine, easy adjustment have for you?

Feelings of Positivity

Although there is an indisputable connection between emotional and mental health and possessions, many individuals don't often consider them to be related. Studies have indicated that organizing your closet can improve mental clarity and peace of mind. And when you consider it, it does make total logic. When did you last organize the stuff in your storage shed or spare room? After it was all over, how did you feel? It normally feels quite relieving and peaceful to the mind. Research has confirmed that this is a positive feeling. Give or discard anything unless you use, love, or need it.

Better Health

Though it might make you uncomfortable to think about it, getting rid of some duties and practicing mental minimalism might also positively affect your physical health. Many individuals overcommit and, driven by fear, accept everything, even when their schedule becomes too full and their well-being suffers. How might reducing one's intake look? Could you sleep a little longer? Could you take better care of your family and yourself? You may prioritize your body's health differently when you reduce the items in your calendar that are stressful or unneeded, as well as the clutter in your life.

A Life with More Freedom

Discovering how much you possess, wish to own, or save up to acquire is absurd if you take a closer look at the matter. Consider the liberating effect of committing your time to something you genuinely desire rather than a property you are trying to impress someone with. You won't feel as pressured to put in long hours at a job you detest to obtain the money to purchase items if you start to value them less.

Reduced Stress

Imagine a future in which you don't have to go to work and come home to unnecessary clutter, don't have to wake up early on the weekends to accomplish things you don't feel like doing and don't have to report to a job you detest every day. This is only a small portion of what minimalism has to offer.

Increased Self-Belief

You may think that owning the newest car is necessary to feel good about yourself or that it is improper to not be up to date with fashion. But supposing you might live a fulfilling life without these extras? Living on less offers you unanticipated benefits. You'll start to feel more confident in yourself, and it won't have anything to do with your possessions.

Greater Life Purpose:

You might be shocked to learn that you have a renewed feeling of purpose when you take the time to eliminate the extra things and activities. You'll be inspired to accomplish your goals because you know where you're going and aren't confused. Less obligations allow you to focus more on the things that count in life.

Conserving Cash

Cutting back on activities and purchases will help you have a little extra cash. There will be fewer eating out, impulsive purchases, and worries. The best part is that you can afford to buy what you want when the time comes since you have extra money. This feature piques the interest of many novices in the minimalism movement. When your income increases, falling into a spending rut might be simple. You'll learn via minimalism that your success is not based on the possessions you own.

Better Connections

Many are trapped in competing with their friends and family over who has the newest smartphone, the nicest automobile, or the largest house. Your relationships will be healthier if you stop trying to impress others around you and instead choose to connect. It can be simple to overlook your family when overly preoccupied with your profession. You can reorder your priorities and rediscover the most important relationships to you through minimalism.

Creating a Simplified Life Plan

You can start creating your simplified life right now, including more things you cherish and find meaningful in this life. Eliminating unnecessary clutter from your life is the first step in a continuous process; it's not the ultimate objective. If you have any doubts, simply consider how much better your life would be if you had fewer possessions.

Effective Work: Utilizing the Whole Clock

Adults typically work 8 to 5 jobs or any other type of job for most of their waking hours. To get the most out of whatever it is that puts bread on the table, you must be completely productive. How, then, do you ensure you are operating at maximum productivity? Here are a few productivity tips to get you going.

*Demolish the Clutter

Keep everything neat and organized on your workstation. Retain what is necessary, file away items that might come in handy later, and dispose of anything that is no longer needed. This will help you concentrate better.

* Take pauses.

It makes sense that taking a little time to unwind at work is now considered normal and acceptable. Take shorter pauses, though, to clear your head and combat fatigue. Strive to work like a sprinter rather than a marathon runner. You will be motivated to exert yourself fully during work by obvious stoppages and pauses. As I've already shown, apply the 80/20 rule to your work to increase productivity by allocating 20% of your work time to tasks that yield 80% of the results and 80% to tasks that yield 20% of the results you want.

* Show heroism at work

The people who enchant everyone and get away with everything are the heroes. Your sincerity, rather than your pretense, will win everyone over. Increase your smiles, lend a hand more, and express your gratitude to those who are kind to you. Your productivity will increase, and your mind will remain stimulated.

* Use Your Smartphone

Although Graham Bell deserves great gratitude, his invention has cost us productivity and comfort of mind. Learn to use your phone sparingly and avoid becoming a pest. The newest generation of smartphones is even riskier, as they can steal your free time and leave you doing nothing at all. Instead of using your phone as a distraction device, use it for communication.

* Adore tidiness

You'll work more productively and harder if your workspace is tidy. In this instance, avoid eating at your desk, remove dirty coffee mugs from your desk, and keep your workspace tidy and smelling good. Keep some fresh herbs or small potted scented plants to make you fall in love with the area every time you take a deep breath.

* Get along well with colleagues

Do you know you spend more time with your coworkers at work than with your family at home? Thus, try being kind to them instead of attempting to be a jerk and uncooperative coworker; offer them some love, and they will undoubtedly return the favor. You can accomplish it by eating in groups, sharing food, interacting with people outside the workplace, etc. Good working relationships with coworkers will undoubtedly increase productivity because they streamline communication and workflow concerns. You won't have to waste valuable working hours to complete tasks behind your coworker's back.

* Persuade without becoming intrusive

It's not always necessary for persuasion to be unpleasant. To gain your superiors' and subordinates' respect and support, constructively drill your thoughts and plans. Develop your interpersonal abilities and be charming when persuading others to establish mutual trust. You can be sure that there won't be many obstacles in your path when you become an expert persuader, which means you won't waste too much time attempting to get other people to agree with or accept your ideas or proposals. Being ready is being godly.

Before beginning any activity, it is necessary to ascertain what must be done. Being organized will keep you one step ahead of your peers and instill confidence. Being organized ensures that there won't be any unforeseen events that could cause work and productivity to suffer. This thus guarantees that everything is planned and prepared for in advance, allowing for a seamless transition between tasks.

Keep to your schedule.

Everybody creates a to-do list, but very few people follow them religiously. Envisioning completed tasks in your head won't make them happen. Ideas need to be put into practice for them to be effective. You won't waste too much time trying out new things when you have a clear to-do list that you follow. Think of it as a template for how you want to do anything you want to achieve. You can concentrate on the things that matter when you don't squander too much time.

You may need to develop the proper habits so that completing tasks naturally comes to you to maintain high productivity.

Section 5. Useful Advice for Streamlining and Organizing Your Area

In today's fast-paced world, it's easy for our houses to get messy and crowded. When accumulating possessions, we quickly become overloaded with stuff we don't need or want. Having a lot of clutter around can make you feel overwhelmed and anxious. You may feel more organized and less stressed by clearing up some space in your life and organizing it. Here are some useful hints to simplify and clean your area.

1. Decide on an objective

Setting a goal is the first stage in decluttering your area. Choose the goal you want to pursue and the area you want to clear out. To make the process feel less demanding, divide it into manageable chunks. You might choose to tidy your kitchen or closet, for instance. When setting aside time for decluttering, keep in mind that it's acceptable to take breaks.

2. Remove everything.

Remove everything from the area you wish to declutter as soon as you've decided on your objective and are prepared to start. This entails clearing out the items from your kitchen cabinets and closet. Nothing should be left behind, not even stuff that is concealed by objects or in corners. After taking everything out, you'll have a clear view of what you have and what has to be thrown out.

3. Divide into groups.

After clearing up your area, group things into appropriate categories. When decluttering your closet, for instance, arrange your clothing into piles according to dresses, t-shirts, jeans, etc. This will enable you to easily determine what you want to keep and discard by allowing you to see how much of each thing you own.

4. Sort through the stuff.

After classifying everything, remove items from each pile one at a time. Consider whether you've utilized each thing in the last year and whether it makes you happy. It's time to let it go if the response is negative. Things that are still in good shape can be donated, and useless stuff can be thrown away.

5. Establish a system

Establish a system for arranging the items left after sorting and decluttering them. This could be labeled boxes to organize your cooking supplies or hangers to divide shirts and pants in your closet. Having a system would improve your area's aesthetics and make it easier to manage in the long run.

6. One coming in, one going out

After decluttering your area, keep it that way by adhering to the 'one in, one out' philosophy. This implies that you should eliminate one item for each item you add to your home. This will stop you from gradually gathering additional clutter.

7. Think about living a minimalist lifestyle.

And lastly, think about living a minimalist lifestyle. This entails paying attention to your things and prioritizing quality over quantity. Decluttering is only one component of minimalism; it's a way of living that values simplicity and clarity in all facets of existence. Adopting minimalism will make your home more orderly and aesthetically beautiful, but it will also make you feel more at ease and in charge of your life.

To sum up, simplifying and clearing up your home can help you live a more stress-free and orderly. You'll be able to clear out the clutter in your house and make a happy, peaceful environment by implementing these useful recommendations. Always remember to go one step at a time and pay attention to the things you surround yourself with.

Section Three
Organizing Your Things: Techniques and Approaches

In this chapter, we'll offer helpful hints and techniques for organizing your belongings and determining what belongs in your possession.

1) Make a list:

Making a list of everything you own is the first step towards simplifying your belongings. You can accomplish this by listing everything you own, room by room. After taking a thorough inventory, you may begin to sift through your belongings and determine which to keep and discard.

2) Begin Little:

You can divide the work of decluttering into smaller parts, like clearing out a room at a time or concentrating on certain belongings, like clothing, books, or kitchenware, to make them easier to handle. Setting a deadline or particular objective for yourself, like clearing out your entire house in a month, can also be beneficial.

3) The "Year-Ring":

The "one-year rule," which says that if you haven't used an item in the last year, you probably don't need it, is an excellent decluttering tactic. It's generally okay to discard anything you haven't used the previous year.

4) Emotional Worth:

A different method of decluttering is to think about an item's sentimental worth. It's best to hold onto sentimental items; if not, it's probably okay to part with them. Consider the sentimental significance of each item as you go through your belongings and make decisions accordingly.

5) Make Sure There's Room:

A more useful decluttering technique is to take stock of your available space. Parting with certain belongings is necessary if your storage isn't large enough to accommodate all you own.

Take into account the limited space and make your decision accordingly.

6) Give With Generosity:

Finding a new home for the things you no longer need is crucial to decluttering. You may declutter your belongings and support your community at the same time by selling or donating stuff.

7) Define Clear Objectives:

Establish measurable objectives for yourself, like cutting down on the amount of stuff you own by a certain percentage or clearing out a specific amount of stuff every day. This will support your motivation and progress.

8) Establish a Timetable:

Make a timetable for cleaning, organizing, and purging your belongings.

9) Consider Your Purchases Carefully:

Consider whether you need the item and whether it will add value and happiness to your life before purchasing.

10) Convey the Art of No:

Saying no to requests that don't fit your minimalist lifestyle is a skill. These could be job or project offers, material belongings, or social invites.

11) Make mindfulness a habit:

You may incorporate mindfulness into your daily life by being mindful and involved in the present moment. Take stock of your belongings and give thanks for what you have instead of dwelling on what you lack.

The minimalist way of thinking for long-term, sustainable travel.

The appeal of perpetual consumption is so strong today that discussing the value of having a minimalist mindset is imperative, particularly for individuals thinking about living a nomadic existence. Setting out on a nomadic adventure without a modest base can cause issues that affect society and the environment, in addition to personal obstacles. The relationship between minimalism and nomadism is essential for ethical and sustainable mobile living—it's not just a question of taste.

Financial Sustainability: Living a nomadic lifestyle without practicing minimalism's discipline can soon deplete one's finances. Even unanticipated relocation and travel expenses add up. You risk experiencing financial instability if you don't practice the cautious prioritization that minimalism advocates.

Environmental Impact: Waste is made worse by constant shopping and throwing away goods when traveling. Reusing, reducing, and recycling are key components of a true minimalist approach—practices crucial for a world facing environmental issues.

Mobility and Efficiency: Nomads must possess agility and be prepared to go at any time. Unnecessary stuff can become a burden and complicate, delay, and increase the expense of changes.

Mental Health: Making decisions about what to keep and throw away regularly might cause decision fatigue. Gradually developing a minimalist mindset leads to more intuitive decision-making, improved mental clarity, and decreased stress.

Being ready and resilient is essential for a nomadic existence, as unforeseen events are inevitable. Minimalists are frequently better equipped to handle surprises because they have developed the ability to distinguish between what is necessary and what is not.

Digital Overwhelm: Minimalism isn't just about physical belongings in the digital era. Digital clutter may be just as daunting, if not more so. It can include excessive programs and copious amounts of data. Since online connectivity is frequently the lifeline for digital nomads, adopting a minimalist approach to digital tools is imperative. A nomadic lifestyle without incorporating minimalism's tenets is like sailing a ship without a compass. It's helpful and vital to cultivate a minimalist attitude for individuals who desire a meaningful, sustainable, nomadic lifestyle.

Take Up a Method

Using the Four-Box Method

Look for a big magic marker and four boxes. Take them into the room you've decided to begin in. In other words, you should arrange four boxes. Trash goes in one, sales go in another, donations go in a third, and anything you intend to keep goes in the final one. Give each box the appropriate label. Pay attention to the visually appealing goods on open shelves and table tops. Sort your belongings appropriately. Proceed to the following room with your four boxes. One may need to be started over if you discover that you have already filled it.

Consider the following questions as you add each item in turn:

Is there anything wrong with this object? Discarding any broken or ragged stuff you may have in your home is necessary. If they aren't important, you don't have to dedicate things to fixing at this point in the decluttering process. If it is something you wish to have fixed, schedule when you will do it. Throw it away if you'll never get around to mending it.

Would I buy this item again if it was broken?

Most people have fallen prey to buying items they rarely use. You might not need them, even though you have already paid for them. You could either sell those items again or just throw them out.

Do I already own one of these?

How many blow dryers are required? What is the required number of tables for the sitting area? Before you take this seriously to decluttering, you should consider these questions and more. You may believe that getting rid of all these duplicates is simple. No, it's not! A garage sale may only sell a portion of the non-damaged products. You have a box for those and can earn some additional cash with them. Some things are worthless and ought to be donated or thrown away.

Is it worth keeping this item?

Countless items could appear appealing or practical. There are no missing ratchet pieces, and the set is beautifully packaged. But why store it if you bought it for a little use? It might do nicely on the market presently. In addition, is there enough room on your shelves or closet for it? Most likely not.

Have I utilized this product in the previous six months?

A good chance exists that you won't require anything if you haven't used it in six months! That is for disposal or selling. Put it in the relevant box, then.

Do these things exist "just in case"?

A truth regarding your sense of security will become clear to you as you progress through the first two rooms. You can find yourself thinking as you sort through your belongings that you should hold onto some "just in case" you need them for _____ in the future. It's also worth noting that these items are inexpensive and unimportant. Consider the problem again and classify it appropriately.

Do these items align with my life goals for the future?

Out of all the questions, this one is the most crucial. Indeed, people frequently talk themselves out of answering certain questions and perhaps sidestepping the issue altogether. But, you must decide for yourself, considering your unwavering resolve to simplify. You need to consider if your decision is sensible and consistent with your goals for your household and family.

There isn't a single justification for maintaining clutter in a home. Therefore, choose to eliminate everything that is rubbish, superfluous duplicates, tattered, or even broken by selling, donating, or throwing it away.

Make your place feel like a home! Make sure everything in your house is safe for your family, your visitors, and your pets, as well as for you. When people are in your home, they should always feel relaxed and at ease. Prioritize your relationships with friends and family over meaningless material belongings. Your pets will also show signs of comfort. Animals are more peaceful in more amiable environments.

Be content, safe, well, and unrestricted. Don't let anything take control of you. This can only be achieved by leading a life devoid of clutter.

The Technique of Time Segmentation

You identified the room with the most clutter while on your house tour. Allocate a duration of approximately five minutes to thirty minutes. Create a "to-do list" for organizing the stuff in that room. Certain rooms might need to be moved from one part to another. It might be your den or workplace space. Even in a computerized world like this, there are still stacks.

You are well aware of the rubbish files you have managed to accumulate if your work is primarily done online. Spend the thirty minutes clearing up each folder one by one. Rename each folder when finished to help you remember which ones are done and which still require work. Following the completion of each time segment, restart your computer. You can prevent computer lag and frozen screens by doing that. Have you never received an apology from a clerk you spoke with stating that their computers are "slow today"? That is a result of their inability to tidy up and restart.

The Garbage Bag Method

This strategy uses two bags.

The Throwaway Items

You will find things that must be thrown away when you search through your most disorganized space, including drawers and closets. You can set out one or two extra bags in addition to your usual disposables on trash day, saving yourself the trouble of filling up twenty bags with trash and dragging the load to the end of your driveway. Naturally, this is a longer-term solution, but it will save you the cost of hiring a rubbish removal agency. Those can add up in cost quickly.

The Giveaways

Do some web research to find charitable organizations that will accept your donations. You should not worry about it being a "legitimate" charity. You will help someone who needs your items.

The "Reversal"

You've altered your mindset by marking your disposables and gift items. It's hardly noticeable when it happens, but after you've donated or thrown out some of your belongings, it becomes more apparent. You now know how to let go of certain tangible possessions. Additionally, you've noticed that your home appears to be more organized and clean. Isn't that a pleasant sensation? Give it another go!

Go back to your home's rooms. Look in your drawers. Once more, ask yourself why you chose to retain each. You'll soon understand that giving up the other things will improve your self-esteem. It improved your capacity for making decisions as well. This liberated conduct has psychological benefits.

Once more, consider the usefulness of everything in your closets and drawers. Choose the ones that make you happy and that you respect. Sort them out carefully. When it comes to clothes, consider which ones go in drawers and which ones you should hang up. Clothes should be stored using the "roll-up" approach. After rolling them up, place them vertically. Don't be afraid to make room. Give yourself kudos for living in such luxury.

The Twelve, Twelve, Twelve Challenge

Include this challenge in your daily routine. This implies that you must find 12 things a day to discard, 12 to donate to charities, and 12 to return to their proper places or your home's rooms. Organizing 36 items in a short amount of time may be fun and interesting with this task. *Make sure the things you have separated are disposed of, donated, or stored neatly. Act quickly to avoid regretting your decision!

Continue doing this until the tops of the furniture and the drawers are empty.

Purging is a positive practice. Additionally, it will be simpler to polish and clean.

Practice Decluttering Your Closet and Drawers:

To begin, hang all your jewelry and clothing in the opposite direction. After wearing them, return them to the drawers and closets in the appropriate order. You should throw away or sell certain items during a garage sale if you haven't used them in four to six months. Save nothing on ill-fitting clothing. Clothes that are torn should not be saved with the idea of repairing them later. "Later" never occurs.

Note: Costume jewelry has a high value. Even though you might not have worn the pin Aunt Jessie gave you very often, it might be beautiful to others. Resellers and merchants are always eager to buy costume jewelry if you don't want to sell it yourself or if you reside in a place where it's not very popular. Many will come running to your house to buy it, no matter how far away!

A two-step process

The KonMari method consists of two steps: arranging and discarding. Discarding is the initial stage in this process.

The secret is visualization.

Kondo advises her clients to try to picture the life they would like to lead.

Retaining and Eliminating

The KonMari Method advises concentrating on stuff you want to keep rather than sorting things according to what you want to throw away. The object you wish to retain should make you happy. If not, throw it away.

The KonMari method has a precise order and is not random. Clothes should be the first thing to go when cleaning and tossing, then books, papers, random objects, and souvenirs. These categories are then broken down into several subcategories. For example, when it comes to clothing, tops should come on first, then bottoms, jackets, socks, etc.

Putting together!

To maintain KonMari, folding is required. Kondo asserts that there is a proper way to fold items.

Confidentiality

According to Kondo, cleaning up should be a private matter in which you carry out your duties. Never discard someone else's belongings without first seeking permission.

Often intimidating

The fact that this approach may seem intimidating to others is one factor contributing to skepticism regarding it. You should only keep absolutely necessary items and discard most of the papers and books in your home. Letters and photos are also included in this.

Easy Storage

According to Kondo, some things must be grouped and stored together. It is not appropriate to leave items strewn about.

Spiritual: You might be surprised to hear that Kondo feels decluttering and cleaning have a spiritual impact. She thinks you can even reduce weight and obtain clear skin with it. Cleaning and decluttering, in her opinion, can open your eyes to a whole new world of happiness and delight.

Chapter 2: Living Simply with Kids

Many parents believe it's hard to lead a simple lifestyle while having kids. Regardless of age, that is just not the case for most youngsters. As a concept they will carry with them for a very long time, minimalism is a fantastic thing to instill in your kids at a young age. Every age group has its own unique set of issues, but it's best to start early.

infants

Although switching to minimalism is easiest when a child is young, you shouldn't make the switch carelessly.

Even if this is your first time being a parent, you will still want to purchase slightly more of everything than you anticipate needing. The worst thing that can happen is to run out of creams or diapers and have to buy more.

Remember that living a minimalistic lifestyle should make your daily life easier rather than more stressful.

Little ones

Toddlers are another excellent choice for an age to transition to minimalism because they still won't remember what it was like to live with more. You will still need to keep toys, educational resources, art supplies, and sporting products around the house for your child to play with. All you have to do is consider what your child needs and when they need it.

Remember that you shouldn't purchase anything for your kids out of greed or as a reward. Invest in items if you genuinely need them to survive or if your child will benefit from them.

Little Children

Children between the ages of 6 and 10 will recognize that they lead a very different lifestyle from other kids, even if they may not be mature enough to fully comprehend why they will be living that way. You must convince kids of this way of life, particularly if it means removing some outdated or damaged toys.

There may inevitably be some crying and arguing, so be ready. You need to remember why you began this journey and believe it would be beneficial. It's okay if you decide to give your child a bit more freedom than you would.

Teens

Even though it may not always seem like it, your children think of human beings. The hardest group to convert to a simple lifestyle will be teenagers. You ought to sit and talk openly with them about your decisions. Give your thoughts on why you believe it might benefit them.

Reassure teenagers that their decision does not imply that they will stop buying things or that they will have to do without, as they tend to draw broad inferences from anything their parents say. Instead, emphasize that you are only purchasing necessities. To help your youngster focus on what to do with money, you may also advise that they find a job.

Myths About Minimalism

Before applying minimalism, you should be aware of certain common misunderstandings about the lifestyle that could lead to a false impression of it all. You must realize that people who practice minimalism may be found in various social classes, ages, sizes, genders, nations, and ethnicities. A burgeoning movement known as minimalism teaches people to live simply, find freedom in the process, and learn to define their lives in ways other than material goods. However, most people still have misconceptions about minimalism despite its rising popularity. Therefore, dispelling a few of the widespread myths around it is crucial.

Prestigious are Minimalists

Probably the most widespread misunderstanding is this one. The reasons for minimalism can differ, even while the way of life is not arrogant in and of itself. Several blogs exist where minimalists brag about how little they own. To claim that there aren't any conceited minimalists among the masses would be untrue; in fact, you can find these individuals in almost every sphere of existence. A sensible way of living, minimalism aims to break the unchecked cycle of accumulation. It's not about lying to people about your minimalist lifestyle or boasting about how little you have.

OCD affects minimalists.

While some people may find minimalism easy, others may find it difficult. Simply put, stuff just seems to gather quickly. The disease known as obsessive-compulsive disorder (OCD) is typified by recurrent and unwelcome thoughts, feelings, sensations, behaviors, or ideas that drive an individual to take specific actions. This misperception is probably because minimalism helps people with OCD. After all, it is a means of promoting relief and relaxation.

Is Minimalism Boring?

Focusing on amazing experiences like travel and adventure and trying new things instead of acquiring stuff is not dull. Minimalists are among the most fascinating individuals you will meet because they are free to pursue their interests and are not constrained by material belongings.

Minimalists prefer white, sterile, basic, chilly, or austere designs.

Adopting minimalism does not entail getting rid of everything fluffy, colorful, and cozy. The practice is unrelated to modern, contemporary design. You can get a lime green couch, utilize a large, vibrant area rug, and paint those walls purple. Reducing waste and undesirable things, people, and influences in your life is the sole goal of minimalism.

Modern hipsters are minimalists.

A few definitions of "hipster" appear when you search for its description. According to some accounts, a hipster keeps up with the newest styles and fads. According to others, it's a subculture of people who respect counterculture, independent thought, and progressive politics. Ideally, these people are in their 20s and 30s. The truth is that your age, income, or political beliefs have no bearing on leading a minimalist lifestyle. Since minimalism is a countercultural ideal, most minimalists are independent thinkers. Beyond this point, there is no direct connection between minimalists and hipsters. Anyone can adopt a minimalist lifestyle, regardless of age, financial status, or place of residence. Furthermore, being trendy is not the core of the lifestyle. It's about simplifying life so you can live each day to the fullest without worrying about many obstacles.

Chapter 3: Techniques for Budgeting and Managing Money

This chapter covers how to build and stick to a minimalist budget. This chapter's techniques and ideas show how minimalism can be used in a practical approach to budget. We will also examine actions and methods that support minimalist budgeting.

Since many bills and other commitments are due every month, it is easiest to think about your income and expenses every month while developing your minimalist budget using these recommendations. Generally, the examples in this book illustrate how budgeting techniques relate to the revenue and expenses of a given month. The same methods and ideas can be used over days, weeks, months, and years.

Examine Your Income

To begin creating your minimalist budget, you must first determine your income.

Use your net monthly income as the input for your budget if you have a regular source of income, such as a job or another source that pays a consistent amount regularly. "Net" refers to the real money in a bank account after deducting all relevant social security and tax amounts.

Your monthly income for budgetary purposes should be the average for the year if you have a seasonal job or work in a sector where the income fluctuates consistently throughout the year (tourist or fishing businesses are ideal examples). Divide your net annual (yearly) revenue by 12 months to find the monthly average.

Use the "worst-case" amount you may receive, such as your lowest monthly salary over the previous year, if your income is inconsistent. It's difficult to forecast how it may vary in the future (for instance, if your pay is based on commissions).

Don't rely on any income that you could receive in the future. You can include inheritances, bonuses, promotions, increases, and lottery wins into your minimalist budget if and when they happen, but not before then.

Of course, your minimalist budget needs to be modified to account for any big changes in your income, whether upward or downward.

You might also think about the following long- and medium-term options to boost your income:

- Concentrate on the aspects of your current work that bring in money. Making the most of your working hours and income opportunities is necessary if you are a self-employed, hourly, or commission worker. If your job pays a salary, consider what makes you eligible for bonuses and raises, and focus on tasks that will result in that extra cash. Avoid getting bogged down in doing things your company doesn't care about; you can assign those things to others.

- You can also apply for a higher-paying job or get a side gig. Consider whether you are utilizing your leisure time effectively and whether it could be better spent working toward a financial goal. One can find numerous websites, such as Indeed.com and Craigslist jobs and gigs, to search for part-time jobs that align with their availability and skill set.

Selling items causing clutter is a smart way to generate extra cash when following the minimalist approach. Consider your possessions, the frequency with which you utilize them, and the level of joy they provide you. Is it possible to convert them into money so you may utilize it for your objectives and the things that are truly important in your life? Using online marketplaces like Craigslist or eBay, you can sell the items you no longer need for a profit.

Chapter 3: Clearing Your Mind

As I mentioned in the introduction, you may be among those who have a great deal of emotional baggage in your life. You become clingy as a result and lose productivity. There's probably a good reason if you've been passed over for a promotion and you notice that people around you receive more cake than they deserve. Being overly emotional or preoccupied leaves little opportunity for creativity or passion, which makes you incredibly dependent and often makes you a bad hire for an employer. It's, therefore, time to dust off the cobwebs and assist yourself in becoming less dependent and cluttered, particularly regarding your emotions.

Adopting the mindfulness posture is among the best approaches to mental cleansing. In plain English, this means that you live in the present moment at all times, not dwelling on the past because it is the past and cannot be returned, and you also don't worry about the future. This may never occur and hasn't happened yet. People resist being ordered to do this, which is an issue. Thus, the best approach to try and introduce you to this minimalist style of thinking would be to set up a specific amount of time each day for practicing meditation. This practice cultivates mindfulness and the ability to return to present-moment thought when problems arise, preventing your mind from becoming overloaded with life's distractions.

Meditation with mindfulness

Pick a place in your house to enjoy uninterrupted quiet for twenty minutes. You should stay somewhere with low outside noise levels and wear comfortable clothing because the last thing you want is to be bothered by a throbbing waistline. Sit upright in your chair. A stiff chair, such as a dining chair, works best; avoid reclining. Maintaining a straight back and a slightly bent head is the goal. Breathing becomes easier for you due to this opening up the airways.

During the first few sessions, keep your eyes closed to prevent your thoughts from straying. Now breathe through your nose until you reach the count of eight, and then exhale while focusing solely on your breath. Repeat the same action. As the air enters your lungs, feel it. Feel the air departing your body while you remain in that instant. You are breathing deeper than usual, which is very beneficial since it allows the sympathetic nervous system to more effectively distribute oxygen throughout the body, something it cannot accomplish when you breathe regularly. If you notice that your thoughts are straying from the breath when you sit and breathe, bring them back to it.

Please don't punish yourself for not being able to focus entirely. You won't be able to do it right away since it takes time to clear your mind of all the concepts that you are accustomed to being there.

Continue doing this for roughly 20 minutes each day. You should use the early morning hours before breakfast as this is tranquil. After you've been doing this for a long, you discover that it benefits you in your daily life by allowing you to take a moment to find a solution rather than becoming overwhelmed by negative or unexpected events. This type of meditation makes you acutely aware of the need to resist letting anything get inside of you. It also improves your ability to concentrate and greatly increases your relaxation. Additionally, I discovered that meditation increases my productivity since it allows me to clear my mind and store thoughts that are more significant than the unrestrained thoughts that could otherwise wander.

I would advise you to practice this every day and to avoid attempting to do it right after eating. Additionally, because this meditation lowers blood pressure and pulse rate, it takes some time for them to return to normal during breakfast. So, be sure to allow yourself enough leisurely time to get up from meditation and continue your day to find answers that work, take a deep breath, and focus on the present moment if you are under extreme stress at work. Also, you'll discover that when your mind isn't overloaded, you tend to take better care of yourself rather than being constantly unproductive due to all those open boxes.

There are moments when it's necessary to embrace your inner child. It's beneficial for you to leap into a puddle and make a splash. This is also beneficial if you want to burst into laughter with your children since you are giving your creative brain a little breathing room. The equal use of the creative and logical sides of the brain was observed in the brain scans of Buddhist monks who practiced meditation. This helps to reduce stress and the negative effects of the outside world, enabling you to be as productive as you were meant to be.

The Pioneer

Simply pick up a backpack and head out into the vast expanse of the universe. Who had not previously considered taking such an action? This is exactly the way an adventurer lives. Books written by dropouts—people who choose to end their lives—are becoming increasingly common in bookstores. To get by, all you need is a little cash, curiosity, and open-mindedness. Taking on work along the road can't be detrimental, as you must make small but consistent progress along the route. You must possess extremely devious thinking skills. This kind of minimalism is so extreme that it even acknowledges the validity of a national homeland. In a sense, the world is home. It is just necessary to consume and possess different items to survive. To adopt such a large lifestyle requires guts. Additionally, to consistently take on new challenges and adventures, meet new people, and explore new places, you must possess certain character traits like curiosity, spontaneity, and a hunger for adventure. But once you've decided to go on such a voyage, I believe you'll return one day with priceless memories.

Perhaps you've observed that you might have more than one guy in you. Furthermore, categorizing and filtering are not relevant here. The minimalist lives I have shown you are meant to serve as inspiration and guidance. Finding the ideal degree of minimalism without sacrificing your enthusiasm for life is ultimately what matters. Ultimately, it's not about cutting corners; rather, it's about embracing the maxim "less is more" in a purposeful and personally appropriate manner. It may seem overwhelming for a novice at first, but as you get the hang of things, the rest will fall into place.

"If every individual renounces accumulating property, then all will have enough."

(Francis of Assisi, 1181–1182, Italian monk and founder of the Order)

Benefits of a minimalist lifestyle

Naturally, there is no way to predict with certainty what benefits may arise from adopting a minimalist lifestyle. But the truth is, there are a lot of benefits that can come with it. In the upcoming chapter, I will explore these benefits further.

More cash

It depends, of course, on your chosen lifestyle and life. However, you will discover your wallet gains when choosing a particular lifestyle. Saving money won't hurt, even though money isn't a major factor in minimalist living. For instance, you may have given up a flashy car or condo and instead saved money for the things that matter, like accumulating less debt. This automatically lowers expenses and gets rid of part of the bill. You won't have to pay for petrol if you don't have a car, and your auto insurance will be canceled. The car repair workshop expenses are also excluded, resulting in significant financial savings. I think adopting a simple lifestyle can only be beneficial financially. How could it possibly get worse?

Joyful

Part of the mindset is being lucky. In addition, other variables are not calculable. Your odds of leading a happier life are higher if you lead a minimalist lifestyle. That has a straightforward explanation. You feel liberated when you live a basic lifestyle. You are free of ballast, and you are free of many other unneeded things as well. Your chances of regaining perspective are higher. Many responsibilities come with possessions; the more you acquire, the more accountability you must exercise. Besides, you can lose more the more you own. The fear of losing grows the more that you stand to lose. You won't need as much to be happy if you have freed yourself from needless items.

You can concentrate on the things that matter because we don't have to look at as many things. Less emphasis is placed on stress and commitments and more on the significant people in your life and your memories and experiences.

Are you still unsure about why I—or anybody else—suggest a tiny, minimalist house? You are aware that you desire every gain in life.

In this small area, you save money, improve the environment, spend more time with your loved ones, and, most importantly, find peace of mind. If living in a tiny house excites you and seems like a practical choice, you should give it some serious thought.

I've compiled a list of some pointers that will help you acclimate to living in a tiny house, whether you already own one or are preparing to move into one. If you wish to live a minimalistic lifestyle, you can apply these tips in any type of residence. I hope it's helpful to you.

- The one-in, one-out rule is a widely accepted guideline that can assist you in keeping track of the number of items you own. Any family member who wants to purchase or add something new must be prepared to part with an existing item. Anything such as a toy, book, or t-shirt can be used for this. The idea behind it is that it makes you think twice before acquiring something new and helps you balance the amount of worldly possessions you own. It will assist you in avoiding clutter addition and overpopulation in a compact house. If followed, this rule can be quite helpful.

- Setting a limit on how much belongings each family member can own is another way to avoid clutter. You could state, for example, that each person can have no more than fifty objects for themself.

These can be switched around, something old can be replaced with something new, or certain objects can be stored, and only fifty can be used at a time. This keeps a mess from accumulating.

- To allocate areas in a house, tiny home builders employ an additional tactic. They designate specific areas of the house with sticky notes. This gives them the first several months to get used to the new space. It also helps you understand that you only need room for a few necessities. You hardly ever used all the large rooms in your enormous house, so they were just a waste of space.

- You can utilize storage containers to provide a basic notion of the space each person is permitted to use for storing their belongings. You can keep everything if it fits within the two bins you supplied. The remaining items must be removed or stored. This is additional advice to help you make more thoughtful and careful decisions about what you want to keep and what you can live without.

- The idea of giving things away once they've fulfilled their purpose for you can likewise be applied. Once you've finished reading a book, give it to someone else to read. It's not necessary to turn your area into a miniature library. Allow someone else to use anything you have finished using and are certain you no longer need. Knowing that something will be useful to someone else is far preferable to throwing it away. This also holds for some items to which you may have sentimental attachments. Even though you're ready to let go of it, you'll feel better knowing someone you can trust takes care of it.

Let's examine practical design advice for creating a tiny house to help you maximize the available space.

- To start, mark down the regions by taping them off when building the house. Use tape to measure how much room you need in the house for sitting, sleeping, wandering about, and other common purposes. An unimaginative design and poor measurements can result in a tiny house construction nightmare. Using the tape, you can determine how much room each area will require and what will allow people to walk around comfortably. You don't have to live in a small area or crouch just because it's small.

Utilize walls to the utmost and most effectively. Making the most use of vertical space is important. Never leave anything lying around on floors or countertops. Provide ways to store and hang everything as close to the walls as possible. To your advantage, this will have a significant impact on how much space you have.

Folding furniture is a valuable asset when constructing a compact home. These days, many options are available for buying pre-made, foldable furniture that only has to be installed. This will be particularly useful for furniture that takes up a lot of room, including dining tables and beds. You can fold them back up after using them as needed when not in use. During the night, when you won't be using the area for anything else, foldable beds only need to be put away. When you wake up, fold it again to make enough room for everything you need. You may also use this option to add a workplace for yourself or study tables for your children. These are incredibly simple to install and assemble. All you need to make it work is wood, hinges, tools, and a lock mechanism.

- Maintain as much ceiling space as you can when creating the house. You have flexibility in using the floor area, but having high ceilings will help you. You can install bunk beds rather than taking up floor space with an enormous bed. You can create the idea of extra space by making your windows larger. Windows not only lets in natural light but also gives the impression that your home is much larger. You may also fit shelves into more space if it is higher.

Select light hues for the walls, furnishings, and other interior décor. Light colors make areas appear larger, while dark hues make them more cramped. Huge mirrors, light walls, and windows will create the appearance of a room that is comfortably spacious. Mirrors are useful because they mirror the area around them, particularly when positioned across from large windows.

- Designate each area as a zone with many uses. You can use your couch as a pull-out bed. Alternatively, you may use the area where your fold-out bed is during the day as a sitting area. Simply reposition the couch or beanbags when you need to sleep at night. You can use the kitchen table as a workspace as well. Making the most of the space around you and being more aware helps.

- Sliding doors and walls are preferable to traditional doors. You may open up the entire area with these, and if you need privacy, you can always close them. Collapsible furniture and doors will make a big impact on your tiny home.

Days 1 through 10

You'll find that the first ten days of minimalism are the most difficult. You will start purging items from your life now and discover a new way of living. This will be a unique experience for you, and you might experience various emotions. If you have to, go gently and take your time. The goal of this challenge is not to force you into a new lifestyle that will make you regret your decisions or feel miserable but rather to properly educate you on how to practice minimalism with a comfortable change. You will see how easy the change may be and how satisfying it can be to be freed from a physical tie as you practice every day as it is offered.

First Day

"There are two paths to wealth: obtaining a great deal and having few desires."

- Koller, Jackie French

Your challenge will begin with a straightforward day. You wish to gather a box that you will store in the middle of your home. Next, you'll put one thing you want to donate inside. You will keep putting one solitary thing into this box every thirty days. You may get rid of thirty things you no longer need from your house by doing this simple task.

You have a full day to come to terms with the fact that these items will be permanently gone if you do it one at a time, making it really easy to let go of them. This act presents two challenges: the first is that you cannot take anything out of the donation bin. It has to remain within once it is there. Second, you have to focus on one task at a time. The point of adopting a new lifestyle is not to become overtaken or startled. Even when you've wanted your home to change quickly for a while, it can still be difficult to witness the entire space transform quickly. You can regret your decision to move too quickly and buy other things to replace the things you had to give up in your house. One by one, the objective is to learn how to live without these things.

As an extra assignment for the first day, you might want to start recording your experiences as you go through this process in a diary you already have lying around your house or in the notepad on your computer. You will be better able to process your changes if you keep a daily journal of your feelings. After that, you can go back to your writing and see why you made the adjustments in case of any difficulties. Make sure to include your pre-challenge feelings and the personal reasons for your decision to begin the challenge. If you ever find yourself in a situation when things are getting tough for you, this will help position you for success. You have now finished the first day's activities for the 30-day challenge.

Day Two

"Living a simpler, lighter life with fewer distractions that impede a high-quality life, as defined uniquely by each individual," is what simplicity entails.

- Linda Breen Pierce

We have too much experience with the adage "out of sight, out of mind." When we accumulate clutter, we frequently push it aside and store it somewhere we can't see it anymore to avoid dealing with the guilt and remorse we experience when we spend money and time on these things. But when we act this way, we avoid dealing with the issue directly. Rather, we ignore it and act as though there was never a problem in the first place.

On the second day, you will go through your junk drawer—or drawers, if you have multiple—and sort things out. These drawers are going to be reclaimed for a reason, and you're going to get rid of anything that makes them into rubbish. This will enable you to thoroughly clean your house, which will have the effect of clearing away all of your darkest secrets. Because the modification is in a hidden place in your house that you won't see immediately but will still be aware of, it's also a great exercise for your second day of the challenge. Consider it an opportunity to physically rewire your house's psyche.

Take everything out of your drawers and give them a thorough cleaning before beginning this exercise. Determine the new function these drawers will serve before moving on. After that, you may start going over everything. Anything that is not helpful or does not make you happy should be discarded. After that, everything that serves the drawer's intended purpose can be carefully put back inside. Include drawer inserts if you want to improve the organizing process. If you don't want them, though, you don't need them. If they make you happier and keep your stuff more organized, buy them.

After you've gone through everything, get rid of whatever you don't need or desire. Junk drawers usually contain minor treasures with little to no use or worth. Throw the rest in the trash unless you have something valuable worth selling. Most of the time, these drawers contain nothing valuable to donate. All of it is just junk wh, which we are too addicted to discard.

Day two is over after cleaning and reusing your junk drawers. You are welcome to write about the encounter and your feelings. Remember that writing about your feelings might aid your emotional processing more than just thinking about them. Additionally, you'll provide a reference point in case the change proves to be emotionally taxing later.

Day Three

"When there is nothing left to take away—rather than when there is nothing more to add—perfection is reached."

- Saint-Exupery, Antoine

You will delve a little bit more into your experience today. Everything that you no longer require will be disposed of. Trash should be done today on any broken repair, objects or items that have been gathering dust while you expect to use them later. All too frequently, we move things about from place to place out of concern that we won't be able to use the benefits they formerly provided without them. Don't let this fear stop you from throwing away things that have outgrown your or any other house.

Take your time as you work on this. Enter each room and dispose of only what you see as trash immediately. Objectively, assess everything you own and honestly ask yourself what should be thrown away. You will delve deeper in the next few days, so there's no need to leaf through the depths now. For now, all you need to do is clear the surface of your house of any rubbish, including the visible areas from the moment you enter.

Everything is easier to do if the rubbish is removed first. It can be liberating to let go of items you have been clinging to due to guilt, fear, or other negative emotions. When we are too guilty to let go of anything, we frequently experience unpleasant emotions whenever we look at it. For instance, you might have bought a living room accessory, decided you didn't need it, or fixed it after it broke, promising yourself you would fix it. If you feel bad about spending your money on it, you could hang onto it or put it in your closet. Since money is just like time, you feel bad about an item because you spent a lot of time and energy getting it, and then it broke or stopped being useful to you. You now feel sad or maybe angry when you think of throwing it away since you think it will resemble lost time. Rather, you hold onto it. You will feel guilty, angry, sad, and maybe many other undesirable or negative emotions every time you look at it now. When this occurs, you have now expended time earning money to obtain an item you no longer desire, and you have also expended time feeling guilty about it. Some people experience this kind of remorse over various possessions for days, weeks, months, or even years. You free yourself from those bad feelings by discarding these things and permanently calling them quits.

Recall that you don't need to go into every room's crevices and discard everything. Not yet, at least. In the next few days, you will have multiple opportunities to discard items you no longer need or want. Remember that you still need to place one thing in your donation box before the third day is out. Then, if you'd like, you can write about what happened to you and how it felt to get rid of these unnecessary and unwanted things from your life and house.

Consumption is countered by minimalism.

Let's look at the words' etymologies. The word minimus, which means tiniest in Latin, is the root of minimalism. Conversely, consumerism originates from the Latin word consumer, combining the words summer, which means to take or buy, and con, which means with or thoroughly.

The tiniest, the simplest, the essence is the focus of minimalism. The main aim of consumerism is group consumption. This is in line with the theory that, although consumerism can help the economy grow overall, it can cause problems when people interpret it as an obsession with acquiring material possessions without question or thought or as a means of sating external or worldly cravings that prevent the fulfillment of inner desires.

This obsession with getting gratification from the outside world can cause someone to spend more than they can afford, accrue debt, and amass clutter—all of which can undermine the goal of improving one's quality of life. Rich and successful people can become wealthy through hard work and good fortune. That same person would probably still feel empty inside or that something is wrong if nothing changed in their inner life.

Compare the distinctions between minimalism and consumerism in the following table.

Minimalism and Consumption

Needs and Wants

Too Much

Superfluous Essential

Eat & Produce

Careless Producer

Self-Deprivation Contribution

Depth and Breadth

Stacking and Prioritizing

Outside Inside

Figure 2: A comparison between minimalism and consumerism

This short observant comment, which came from humorist Robert Quillen, is frequently used by financial gurus and minimalists: "We buy things we don't need, with money we don't have, to impress people we don't like." Sometimes, we don't even know the people we wish to impress!

Reversing consumerism's downward trend can be facilitated by minimalism. Tools and methods acquire meanings when viewed through a consumerist lens. Material goods and money are merely means to an end rather than ends. But as if they were the most significant things in life, consumerism drives us to follow them relentlessly. Adopting a minimalist attitude serves as a reminder of what matters most in life, which is typically not material possessions.

Antoine de Saint-Exupéry stated that "what is essential is invisible to the eye" and that "one can only see rightly with the heart" in his 1943 book The Little Prince.

Through a deep examination of our hearts and minds, minimalism is a tool that enables us to examine our bodies and the world we have built. As we go through each physical thing, we ask ourselves, "Do I need this in my life?" Is this really what my heart longs for? How does it benefit me in my life? Am I obsessive over this? Why am I so invested in this? Do I have positive motivators? Or is it a result of uncertainty, worry, and fear? Should I let it go, what would happen?

There's a well-known adage about ranking necessities first. Here's an updated version of it.

In front of his class, a lecturer places an empty jar on the table. After placing his priceless gold shells adorned with pearls inside, he asks his students if the jar is full. Yes, his class responds.

He then fills the jar with pebbles to cover the gaps between and within the gold shells. When the jar is full, he asks his class. They say "yes."

He then fills the microscopic gaps between the pebbles and the gold shells in the jar with sand. When the jar is full, he asks his class. They say with a strong "yes."

Subsequently, he fills the jar with a glass of seawater and absorbs its contents. At last, he announces that the jar is full.

He explains to the students that the jar stands for life and that the gold shells containing pearls symbolize one's connections, well-being, and hobbies. Even if you remove the stones, sand, and saltwater, your jar will still be full and rich.

The aids or facilitators are the pebbles. They hold the gold shells in place. These are tangible possessions, such as your home, vehicle, employment, clothes, and net worth. It might also involve instruments like minimalism and education.

The fine particles are called sand. If you pour the sand first, there won't be room for the gold shells and pebbles. There won't be room for the gold shells if you arrange the pebbles first. Sort your gold shells first, followed by pebbles, and then leave the remaining sand.

"No matter how full your life may seem, there's always space and time to enjoy the sea with your loved ones," the professor says with a smile in response to a question from one of his students on what saltwater signifies.

What are your gold shells, you ask? What necessities do you have? How are things going with your gold shells? Who are the pearls you speak of? In life, who do you value most?

Upon closer inspection, you may need to reevaluate your life priorities if you realize that you are giving your pebbles, sand, and seawater more importance than anything else. It's not just about collecting stones in life. It concerns how stones fit between pearls and gold shells in your jar.

Consumerism is like a jar with stones, sand, and saltwater, holding one or two gold shells or none at all. You can empty your jar and arrange your belongings properly when you practice minimalism. For example, arrange your gold shells first before anything else.

This brings us to prioritization, which is the functional definition of minimalism.

Resource allocation under minimalism is deliberate and prudent.

An organization, such as a corporation or an individual, must manage three resources. They are energy, money, and time.

Figure 3: The Project Management Triangle, or the Three Resources of Individuals and Groups

From a managerial standpoint, a company's or business's expansion entails maximizing or conserving time, money, and energy. This is how businesses increase the amount of goods and services they offer. This is the way that consumerism continues.

As individuals, what if we, too, practice minimalism to save and maximize our time, money, and energy?

Take a moment to review your life. In what ways do you think your spending is excessive? Do you find yourself working too hard to make ends meet so you can afford the things you believe you need? Do you labor to pay off bills that never go away, no matter how much money you make? Do you overspend on impulse purchases, sales, or possibly to support a vice or other addiction? Do you commute or drive for hours daily, expending excessive energy?

How do you direct your limited resources (money, time, and energy) toward more fruitful endeavors or pursuits that make your heart dance and sing rather than pound and sag?

When was the last time you spent quality time with your family or friends resting in the sun at the beach or the sea?

As you begin your journey toward minimalism, you can consider all of these reflection topics.

Minimalism encourages you to make a conscious effort to utilize resources sensibly and to make room for what you need. In the process, it counteracts the negative effects of consumerism and restores equilibrium in your life, enabling you to find happiness and fulfillment outside of material possessions.

But you don't want to become a complete minimalist when you wake up one day. Since it's a lifelong endeavor, the process never truly finishes. This concludes our discussion on minimalism as a way of life.

Obtain Mental Clarity

Among the less obvious advantages of minimalism is mental clarity. It's commonly believed that your workstation symbolizes your emotional condition. The latter is probably cluttered as well if the former is disorganized. A clear desk is a sign of a clear mind.

However, there are disagreements over the best type of desk. Proponents of crowded workstations included luminaries like Thomas Edison, Albert Einstein, and Steve Jobs. Advocates claim that the disarray stimulates their creative thinking. Even a study backs up this assertion.

Some historical figures have had chaotic workspaces, which has led to the belief that disorganization is a sign of genius. However, others who live in chaos claim that a tidy workstation is a sign of sloth.

Your surroundings can help you be more creative, but you can also become more creative via practice. If there isn't a lot of clutter, you can use the cleaning time to practice. This time can also be used to explore and learn new things.

It's also important to remember that most individuals find clutter distracting. Many people struggle to concentrate on their work because they need to locate things or feel they should clean up. On the other hand, a tidy desk makes it easier to notice what has to be brought out. You'll be more likely to put away the items you use when you become accustomed to seeing your desk.

It takes more than just clearing clutter from your workstation and other surfaces to achieve mental clarity. Minimalism is avoiding conflict, recognizing advertisements for what they are not, using social media less, and screening your ideas. You are also a mindfulness expert. Using these can reduce the possibility of mental clutter being just as annoying as physical clutter.

Boost Well-being

Food can also be a type of clutter. Known by many as junk food, this comprises processed meat, candy bars, potato chips, and soft drinks. You'll learn more about these bad foods—many mislabeled as nourishing—in Chapter 7.

You'll cut junk food out of your diet since it's clutter. Selecting the nutrient-dense variety lowers your chance of acquiring diseases, including obesity, diabetes, and high blood pressure. A healthy diet might help reduce symptoms and indicators if you have a serious ailment. It helps to avoid developing new issues as well.

Stress is another risk factor for developing and exacerbating diseases like poor eating. Fortunately, a lot of minimalist practices reduce stress. One example would be to decrease online interactions. Getting enough sleep and expediting your morning routine can also help you be calm and productive at work rather than worrying about being late. Minimalism reduces stress and frees up time for soothing pursuits like reading a book, visiting an amusement park, or getting a massage.

Instead of cleaning and becoming sidetracked, you may utilize the time you've saved to improve your relationship with your loved ones. It's not always the case that minimalism suggests shrinking your personal and professional networks. In any case, you will inevitably meet new individuals in the future unless you decide to live alone on an island. They might be new family members, coworkers, or neighbors. You can employ minimalism in your relationships by strengthening bonds with those closest to you rather than interacting with a few people.

Strong relationships provide you with a wealth of moral support. There are emotional benefits to this. Additionally, having that support is helpful during trying times, such as when you have a significant illness or trouble with your body image. When others want you to stay well, you can feel accountable if you're skipping out on exercise and eating a healthy diet.

When it comes to avoiding addiction or overcoming it, moral support is really important. However, minimalism reduces your chance of developing an addiction to a substance or activity by teaching you to set boundaries.

Boost Productivity

A tidy workspace and a clear head are two things that increase productivity. Your efficiency is enhanced by minimalism in another sense as well.

Have you read any accounts of people performing extraordinary feats without arms? Many of them manage to eat, bathe, clean, and write by themselves, even in the absence of hands. Then there are people with physical disabilities who paint, fire arrows, play musical instruments, and even pilot a plane. Even though technology aids some of them, it's still important to see how they use different bodily parts to hold objects like food, paintbrushes, and other items. How about you? Are you also adept at holding objects with your lips or toes?

Numerous obstacles in your path force you to adjust. You could find it difficult to use fewer items than you are now utilizing for the time being. You keep employing a few things again as a means of adapting. The repetition appears to be a drawback at first. But eventually, you'll become an expert. That's what happened to those with physical disabilities.

It should come as no surprise that many people who genuinely represent the thinking of the consumer are exceedingly delicate. Anything could trigger them. You can accept life as it is if you begin to peel away all of that and concentrate on what you need and who you truly are.

Not everything in life is simple and easy. You already know that I'm sure. You can frequently get knocked down and hauled by the hair by life. Life isn't fair, but you can view things in perspective if you have the correct attitude and realize that life isn't just about you. To react effectively, you don't have to act like a chicken with its head chopped off and think everything is about to end. It's not. You are not where the world starts or ends.

The less is more route.

Recognize that when you adopt the less-is-more philosophy, you reframe every aspect of who you are, ultimately affecting your self-worth. Because you can contribute more to others, you value yourself more. You begin to believe that giving to others and being interconnected are the key components of what makes you valuable since those are the fundamental components of love.

Love is the pursuit of others, not the pursuit of oneself. Love is patient because it doesn't think the world revolves around it or that it is everything. Love is selfless since it prioritizes and seeks out others. It doesn't pretend to be something it isn't.

You should be familiar with this if it is. This comes from a Western spiritual tradition, but it has many Eastern parallels as well since, in the end, the truth about ourselves is that we must be selfless in some way to be truly happy.

Humility is one of the shapes and entrances it takes. It doesn't have to be about you, or it's not about you. In the end, nobody seems to care. They're preoccupied with their own needs. You have so much love to give when you start to become the person who understands all of this, and ironically, people start cherishing you because you're the one who sticks out from the crowd and starts giving when everyone else is busy receiving.

In summary, the less is more approach has everything to do with mindset and has nothing to do with poverty. It also has much to do with discovering the true, worthwhile things in life. Ideas that frequently materialize as objects are life's true, valuable things. These concepts include Selflessness, giving others time, thinking of others, showing patience, and adopting a child's viewpoint on life.

When was the last time you had Christmas fever? I'm thinking about something simpler, like when you were six years old, not just Black Friday or Cyber Monday deals. You asked your mother when Christmas would arrive in the middle of June because you couldn't wait to see Santa Claus, decorate the tree, or go ice skating in your town or city. Warm hugs from a family who travel from all across the nation are something else you anticipate.

When was the last time you experienced such excitement? I need you to reclaim that frame of mind because, in our more consumer- and product-driven modern world, one of the first things people tend to lose is a sense of anticipation. We let go of that because, in the end, what counts is the process that made Christmas such a lovely and breathtaking event—not the trinket you end up with when you unwrap that shiny piece of paper covering your gift. You have to read into it, but that's precisely one of the things we lose in today's society.

One of the things that makes life worthwhile is the feeling of anticipation, which you will rediscover when you adopt the philosophy that less is more. You begin to value an item's intrinsic value rather than the money you paid for it, or the fact that you waited for it to arrive, or that you solved an issue by using it and then observed the issue resolve itself.

That feeling of astonishment reappears, and it's fantastic. It fills in many gaps in your life rather than acquiring something with the hope that it will function as promised, and when it does, you stop thinking about it altogether.

You proceed to the following issue, and so on. Life is not a festival anymore. It feels like you're racing through life.

Are you going to?

For what reason do we watch TV? For us, what is in it? While it could be entertaining, why do we require five hours of entertainment every day? Are there other entertaining activities we may engage in that will significantly improve our quality of life? Reading amuses. Plus, it's one of the greatest methods to learn new skills. Making art is fun. If other people appreciate and find enjoyment in your work, then they, too, can gain from it. Exercise keeps us fit and healthy and can also be amusing. Writing is a fun activity that can also help you tell a story that inspires or amuse others. Watching television is a self-centered kind of amusement. Your five hours of television a day help who else?

It's a huge amount of time—five hours a day! Remember that you have four minutes. I will bet that not even half of Americans work out for five hours a week. Most of us have reasons why we can't spend more time being active. How will we find five hours a week to go out and perform cardio when we have kids, jobs, and hectic lives? Keep your TV time if you must, but if you watch for four hours a day rather than five, you'll have more time for Planet Fitness' elliptical and Game of Thrones. That was just one hour ago. What if you gave up watching TV completely? You would gain thirty-five and a half hours a week, or five hours daily. What would you do if you had an additional five hours every day? Every day, you would have an hour to dedicate to anything else you choose. You could work out for an hour, read or study, acquire a new skill or language, create art or something useful for society, or any combination.

Each month, watching TV costs money. Although $60 to $80 a month might not seem like much, it adds up. Overindulging in TV viewing can also be harmful to your health. Fitness instructor Jack LaLanne, a global celebrity, held that the human body ages and becomes frail due to underuse rather than abuse. In addition, Jack LaLanne was well-known for breaking records with his strength well into his sixties and seventies. Until he was ninety-nine, he worked out every day. Do you know what a Smith machine is? A leaping Jack? Has someone ever said, "That guy is jacked!" to you?"? LaLanne, Jack. If he is correct and inactivity causes the body to deteriorate, watching TV is the best way to age oneself.

Television's impact on your clock—it takes away hours of your life and fills them with nothing—may be worse than the physical effects it has on you. Watching television won't likely teach you anything unless you solely watch documentaries. Anything we learn from documentaries won't likely stick with us for very long, in my opinion. To what extent do we remember the few facts we learn from documentaries? Despite having viewed hundreds of them—and continuing to do so online—I cannot think of a single item I have learned from them. Even "non-fiction television" serves more as a source of amusement than knowledge. I'm not here to be the TV Police; rather, I'm here to advise you to limit the amount of time you spend watching TV because, when you're 85 years old, you won't look back on your life and regret seeing more Sons of Anarchy.

Computer Games

TV shows and video games go hand in hand. They are just as addictive, if not more so. I was raised on video games. When my older brother was ten, my parents purchased him an original Nintendo Entertainment System. Over the years, we played that NES a lot together, and when I turned ten, my parents gave me a Super Nintendo Entertainment System. I purchased multiple new video game systems, including handheld ones, for ten years following that. Before my westward voyage, I was still playing many video games after giving away my systems and games. Even though I thought I would miss my games at the moment, I still enjoyed playing them. But you know what? Never have I.

We'll refer to this phenomenon as the World of Warcraft Effect because it has existed for years. The theory behind the World of Warcraft Effect—that many young men were becoming so dependent on the video game that they were neglecting almost every other part of their lives, including their relationships with significant others and frequently even their jobs—is probably more of a joke than anything else.

Even though I've never played World of Warcraft, I found this fascinating when I first heard about it. I recall perusing numerous articles and first-person narratives from individuals engrossed in the game. Although I don't have a moral problem with people playing video games, there is a problem if you play them so frequently and excessively that it's affecting your relationships and career. You're looking into a real black hole if you're so dependent on something that your girlfriend is about to break up with you, and your job is about to fire you. Video games can be fun, but they won't teach you anything, they won't earn you money, they won't provide you with much life or love advice, and playing them won't help anyone or improve the world. It's meaningless entertainment. They demand money and time from you and offer little in return.

You'll have a lot more time on your hands to accomplish something that will amuse you and benefit the world if you restrict your daily television and video game consumption to an hour or two. You will find something that resonates with you, given the extra time you will have from living a minimalist lifestyle, so don't panic if you haven't found the thing or things that best suit you. I have a strong affinity for juggling. After quitting smoking, I began juggling a few months later. Juggling has several benefits: enjoyable, inexpensive, free, constantly rewarding, and portable—you can juggle almost anything. In and of itself, juggling improves balance and coordination and practically creates ambidexterity. A skilled juggler can wow an audience with their talent, and others find some joy and entertainment in watching.

What Is Minimalism, Chapter 1?

At this point, you might wonder, "Well, what exactly is this, and how do I do it?" Living simply is a way of life. It's about being content with what you have, not only about simplifying your life and cutting back on consumption. In this book, you will get advice about minimalism, how to live a minimalist lifestyle, how to become a minimalist, and how to maintain a minimalist lifestyle.

As with many things, there are varying degrees of intensity. It's not impossible to learn something from this book, even if you don't want to fully commit to it and alter your lifestyle. There are universal lessons in this book that anyone can apply. Everyone wants to consume less, and generally, everyone wants to be happier. This is advantageous not just for the environment but also for your wallet! Together, let's engage in a little workout. I want you to imagine what a minimalist would look like. What comes to mind? How do they appear? What kinds of activities are they interested in? And what about other aspects of them? Most people associate minimalists—or those with a minimalist look—with survivalists, typically found in remote areas surviving off the land. In actuality, a minimalist is an individual just like you and me. They are average people who engage in most of the same activities. The primary distinction is their decision to modify their lifestyles by reducing consumption and finding contentment in what they already have.

Many people are curious as to how happiness and material possessions are related. Numerous studies have consistently demonstrated that possessing many personal belongings does not necessarily mean greater happiness. Research indicates that your happiness doesn't increase with wealth once you have enough to cover your fundamental necessities, which include food, drink, shelter, protection, etc.

Just keep in mind that internal motivation is required for any kind of lifestyle adjustment. You are the only one who can genuinely inspire yourself to make changes; no one else can. Two categories of motivators exist. There are two types of motivators: internal and external. A vast range of things can serve as external motivators. They could be anything from your pals advising you to get pizza for lunch to your mother instructing you to tidy your room. They could be understated or overt. There are also internal motivators. These are the more potent kinds of incentives. These originate internally. Usually, a realization is the first step. It occurs when you glance at your room and decide it must be cleaned because it is messy. It occurs when you look at a piece of pizza and decide to purchase it for yourself since it looks so nice. Inception, a well-known film, is even based on this. Everything revolves around the idea that you will be far more driven and inclined to carry it through if an idea originates from you. It's a great movie for those who haven't watched it!

If you want to modify your lifestyle for the better, you need to be motivated from the inside out since that's what will stick with you. Remember why you're doing these things and what inspired you to lead this lifestyle while reading this book.

It's the minimalist method. It's the process of making your life more organized. Making the most of the things you do and getting rid of the useless stuff is the goal of minimalism.

Some individuals think that the main component of minimalism is getting rid of stuff. That is an extremely gloomy perspective. Practicing minimalism is about clearing out things, people, and ideas that don't add value to your life to make room for calm, relaxation, and peace of mind.

Many pointless things in our lives are not useful. Some thoughts go about in our heads but never come to pass. Our hearts are ablaze with wants we are not prepared to give in to. Some cling to us like leeches and are not welcome. We choose to overlook all of these things for so long that they cease to be essential components of who we are. They nonetheless, though, are a part of us.

A method to recognize all of these things and methodically and surgically eliminate them from life is through minimalism. Being minimalistic inherently raises awareness. You start to realize how significant everything is around you and how little other people are. The essential ones can be kept, and the others can be deleted.

For some people, the absurd thought of fleeing is a constant source of anxiety. Running away has no resolution and isn't a long-term fix, even though it also refers to escaping from things. Gathering pointless items is a habit that must be carefully broken. It doesn't just happen by escaping life. Living on your terms and adopting a minimalist lifestyle are simple solutions to complex life problems.

You can shape your life to be the way you want it to be by implementing minimalism. You deliberately choose what you need rather than what you want. You begin to live with a purpose and cease to live based on desires. You can devote all your attention to the connections that matter most to you when you lead a minimalistic lifestyle. It assists you in lowering your needs, giving you more time and energy to work towards your objectives.

The idea of minimalism is freeing. It aids in your escape from the pointless rat race. You can discover a reason to run and quit following the crowd.

www.ingramcontent.com/pod-product-compliance
Lightning Source LLC
Chambersburg PA
CBHW052145110526
44591CB00012B/1872